# Easy Steps to Chinese for Kids

## Za
### Textbook
英文版

# 轻松学中文
## 少儿版

**Yamin Ma**
**Xinying Li**

北京语言大学出版社
BEIJING LANGUAGE AND CULTURE
UNIVERSITY PRESS

**图书在版编目（CIP）数据**

轻松学中文：少儿版：英文版. 2a ／ 马亚敏，李欣颖编著.
－北京：北京语言大学出版社，2011.11（2017.5重印）
（轻松学中文）
ISBN 978−7−5619−3170−7

Ⅰ.①轻... Ⅱ.①马...②李... Ⅲ.①汉语−对外汉语教学
−教材 Ⅳ.①H195.4

中国版本图书馆CIP数据核字（2011）第211708号

| | |
|---|---|
| 书　名 | **轻松学中文：**（英文版）少儿版 课本.2a |
| 责任编辑 | 王亚莉　孙玉婷 |
| 美术策划 | 王　宇 |
| 封面设计 | 王　宇　王章定 |
| 版式设计 | 北京鑫联必升文化发展有限公司 |
| 责任印制 | 周　燚 |

出版发行　北京语言大学出版社
社　　址　北京市海淀区学院路15号　邮政编码：100083
网　　址　www.blcup.com
电子邮件　escbooks@blcu.edu.cn
电　　话　编辑部 010−8230 3647/3592
　　　　　发行部 010−8230 3650/3591/3651/3080
　　　　　读者服务部 010−8230 3653/3908
网上订购　010−8230 3668 service@blcup.net
印　　刷　北京联兴盛业印刷股份有限公司
经　　销　全国新华书店

版　　次　2011年11月第1版　2017年5月第7次印刷
开　　本　889mm×1194mm　1/16　印张：6.25
字　　数　30千字
书　　号　ISBN 978−7−5619−3170−7/H.11216
　　　　　07800

©2011 北京语言大学出版社

*Easy Steps to Chinese for Kids* **(Textbook)2a**
Yamin Ma, Xinying Li

| | |
|---|---|
| Editor | Yali Wang, Yuting Sun |
| Art design | Arthur Y. Wang |
| Cover design | Arthur Y. Wang, Zhangdig Wang |
| Graphic design | Beijing XinLianBiSheng Cultural Development Co.1td |

Published by
Beijing Language & Culture University Press
No.15 Xueyuan Road, Haidian District, Beijing, China 100083

Distributed by
Beijing Language & Culture University Press
No.15 Xueyuan Road, Haidian District, Beijing, China 100083

First published in November 2011
Printed in China
Copyright © 2011 Beijing Language & Culture University Press

E-mail:escbooks@blcu.edu.cn
Website: www.blcup.com

# ACKNOWLEDGEMENTS

A number of people have helped us to put the books into publication. Particular thanks are owed to the following:

- 戚德祥先生、张健女士、苗强先生 who trusted our expertise in the field of Chinese language teaching and learning

- Editors 王亚莉女士、唐琪佳女士、黄英女士、孙玉婷女士 for their meticulous work

- Graphic designers 王章定先生、李越女士 for their artistic design for the cover and content

- Art consultant Arthur Y. Wang for his professional guidance and artists 陆颖女士、孙颉先生、陈丽女士 for their artistic ability in beautiful illustration

- 范明女士、徐景瑄、左佳依、田沐子、南珊、陈子钰 who helped with the sound recordings and 徐景瑄 for his proofreading work

- 刘慧 who helped with the song recordings

- Chinese teachers from the kindergarten section and Heads of the Chinese Department of Xavier School 李京燕女士、余莉莉女士 for their helpful advice and encouragement

- And finally, members of our families who have always given us generous support

# INTRODUCTION

- The primary goal of this series *Easy Steps to Chinese for Kids* is to help total beginners, particularly children from a non-Chinese background, build a solid foundation for learning Chinese as a foreign language.
- The series is designed to emphasize the development of communication skills in listening and speaking. Recognizing and writing characters are also the focus of this series.
- This series employs the Communicative Approach, and also takes into account the unique characteristics of the children when they engage in language learning at an early age.
- Each lesson has a song using all the new words and sentences.
- Chinese culture is introduced in a fun way.
- This series consists of 8 colour books, which cover 4 levels. Each level has 2 colour books (a and b).
- Each textbook contains a CD of new words, texts, listening exercises, *pinyin* and songs, and is supplemented by a workbook, word cards, picture flashcards and a CD-ROM.

# COURSE DESIGN

- **Character** writing is introduced in a step-by-step fashion, starting with strokes, radicals and simple characters.
- *Pinyin* is not formally introduced until Book 3a, as we believe that too-early exposure to *pinyin* may confuse children who are also learning to read and write in their mother tongue.
- **Language skills in listening and speaking** are the emphasis of this series, and the language materials are carefully selected and relevant to children of this age group.
- **Motor skills** will be developed through all kinds

# 简介

- 《轻松学中文》（少儿版）旨在帮助那些母语为非汉语的初学儿童奠定扎实的汉语学习基础。
- 本套教材的目标是通过强调在听、说能力方面的训练来培养语言交流技能。同时，识字和书写汉字也是这套系列教材的重点。
- 教材中采用了交际法，并在课程设计中考虑到儿童在这个特定的年龄段学外语的特点。
- 每课配有一首歌曲，用歌曲的形式把当课的生词和句子唱出来。
- 中国文化的介绍是通过趣味性的活动来实现的。
- 本套教材分为四级，每级分为a、b两本彩色课本，共8本。
- 每本课本后附有一张CD，录有生词、课文、听力练习、拼音和歌曲。课本还另配练习册、词语卡片、图卡和CD-ROM光盘。

# 课程设计

- 汉字书写先从笔画、偏旁部首和简单汉字着手。
- 拼音从3a才开始系统介绍，因为小朋友过早学拼音可能会影响他们母语的阅读和书写能力的培养。
- 听、说技能的培养是本套教材的重点，所选语料适合小朋友的年龄段及其兴趣爱好。
- 小朋友的手部握笔掌控能力的培养是通过各种精心设计的有趣的活动来实现的，这些活动可以是画线、画图、上色、描红、做手工等。
- 认知能力的培养是儿童早期教育的一个重点。

of fun and interesting activities, including drawing lines and pictures, colouring, tracing characters and making handicrafts, etc.

- **Cognitive ability** is a very important aspect of early schooling. By understanding the world around them through shapes, colours, directions, etc., children may find Chinese language learning more exciting, fun and relevant.
- **Logical thinking and imaginative skills** are nurtured through a variety of activities and practice, which create space for children to develop these skills as early as possible.
- **A variety of activities,** such as songs, games, handicrafts, etc., are carefully designed to motivate the children to learn.
- **Hands-on practice** is carefully designed throughout the series to make learning meaningful and enhance retention.
- **The pace** for developing language knowledge and skills takes a gradual approach, which makes it easy for children to build a solid foundation for learning Chinese.

- 通过图形、颜色、方向等的学习，小朋友认识了他们周边的世界，汉语学习也变得活泼、有趣，小朋友还能活学活用。
- 通过一系列精心设计的活动和练习，培养小朋友的逻辑思维和想象力。
- 各种各样、丰富多彩的活动，比如歌曲、游戏、手工等，都是为了激发小朋友学习汉语的积极性。
- 培养动手能力的练习贯穿始终，使小朋友学起来更有意思，也有助于他们掌握和巩固新学的内容。
- 学习的节奏由慢到快，循序渐进，使小朋友轻松打好汉语学习的基础。

# COURSE LENGTH

# 课程进度

- This series is designed for young children or primary school students.
- With one lesson daily, primary school students can complete learning one level, i.e. two books, within an academic year.
- Once all the eight books have been completed, learners can move onto the series *Easy Steps to Chinese* (Books 1-8), which is designed for teenagers from a non-Chinese background.
- As this series is continuous and ongoing, each book can be taught within any time span according to the students' levels of Chinese proficiency.

- 本套教材专为幼儿或小学生编写。
- 如果每天都有汉语课，大部分学生可以在一年内学完一个级别的两本。
- 如果学完四级8本，学生可以继续学习同一系列的为非华裔中学生编写的《轻松学中文》（1—8册）。
- 由于本教材的内容是连贯的，教师可根据学生的水平来决定教学进度。

# HOW TO USE THIS BOOK

**1**

New words are introduced through pictures.

**2**

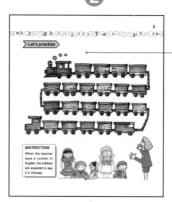

The teacher is encouraged to use different ways to help the children say the new words correctly and memorize their meanings.

**3**

The texts are presented in forms of phrases, sentences or conversations.

**4**

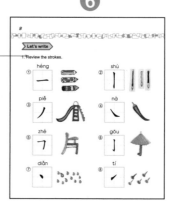

The songs will help the children memorize the new words and sentences in a fun way.

The children develop their speaking skills through picture talks.

**5**

**6**

The children are encouraged to review the strokes, which is the basic training for writing characters later on.

**7**

Fun activities are designed to reinforce and consolidate language learning.

**8**

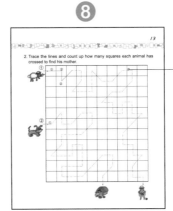

Such activities provide opportunities for the children to develop their logical thinking and imagination.

**9**

Such exercises are designed for the children to practise writing characters.

**10**

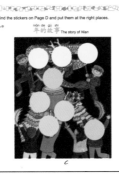

This section of Chinese culture can be introduced whenever the need arises.

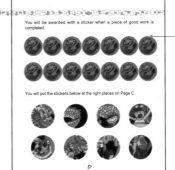

Stickers are given to the children when a good piece of work is completed.

# CONTENTS 目录

> **Let's learn new words**  01

① 
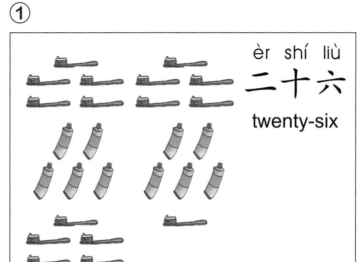

èr shí liù

二 十 六

twenty-six

②

sān shí bā

三 十 八 thirty-eight

③

sì shí

四 十 forty

## Let's practise

### INSTRUCTION

When the teacher says a number in English, the children are expected to say it in Chinese.

**Let's use new words**  02

èr shí yī　　èr shí èr
二十一、二十二、

èr shí sān　　èr shí sì
二十三、二十四、

èr shí wǔ　　èr shí liù
二十五、二十六、

èr shí qī　　èr shí bā
二十七、二十八、

èr shí jiǔ　　sān shí
二十九、三十，

sì shí　　sì shí
四十、四十。

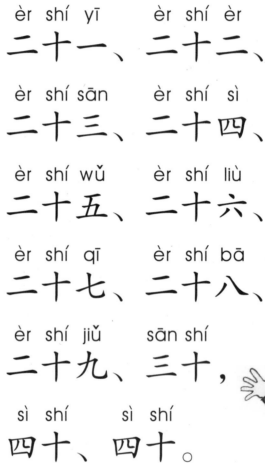

Let's sing 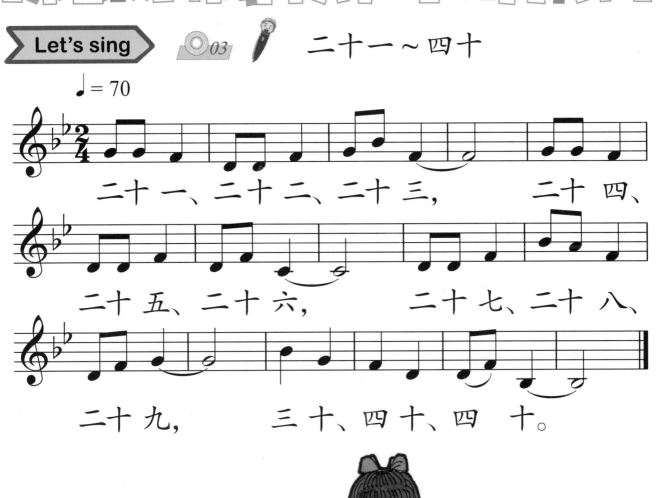 03 🖊 二十一～四十

♩ = 70

二十 一、 二十 二、 二十 三, 　　二 十 四、

二十 五、 二十 六, 　　二十 七、 二十 八,

二十 九, 　　三 十、 四 十、 四 十。

## Let's say it

Find the items listed on the right, count up and say the numbers in Chinese.

Let's write

1. Review the strokes.

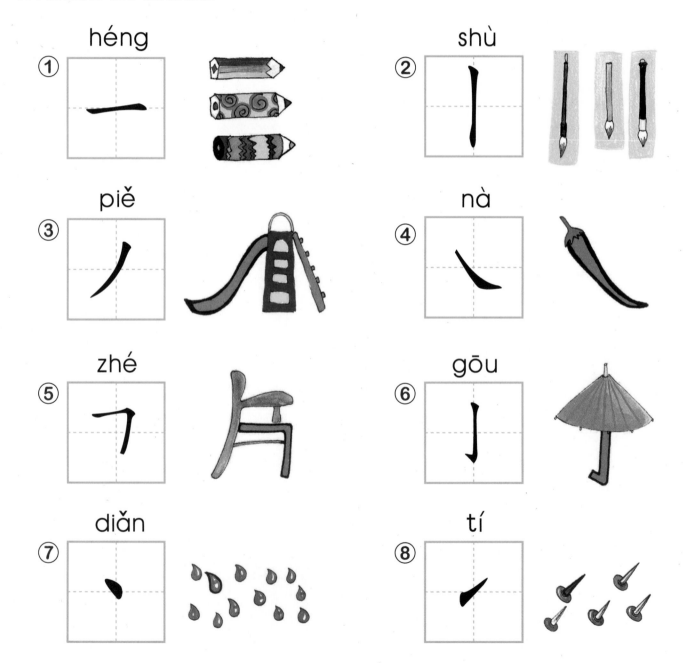

héng
① 一

shù
② 丨

piě
③ 丿

nà
④ ㇏

zhé
⑤ ㇆

gōu
⑥ 亅

diǎn
⑦ 丶

tí
⑧ ㇀

## 2. Find the strokes and trace them with the colours given.

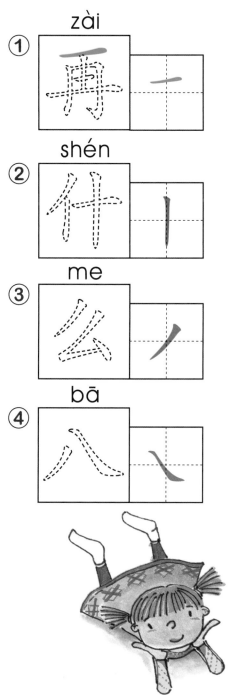

① zài

② shén

③ me

④ bā

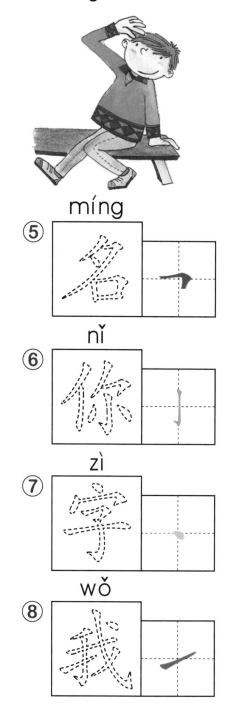

⑤ míng

⑥ nǐ

⑦ zì

⑧ wǒ

> Let's play

10 + 9 = ?

shí jiā jiǔ děng yú
十加九 等 于……
plus    equal to

shí jiǔ
十九

**INSTRUCTION**

When the teacher says any two numbers, the children are expected to add them up and say the answer in Chinese as quickly as possible.

Some examples:

① 10 + 9 =

② 30 + 7 =

③ 25 + 3 =

④ 15 + 5 =

⑤ 30 + 1 =

⑥ 10 + 16 =

⑦ 12 + 10 =

⑧ 23 + 12 =

1. Trace the dotted line in one go.
2. Count up in Chinese how many squares the leaf has covered.

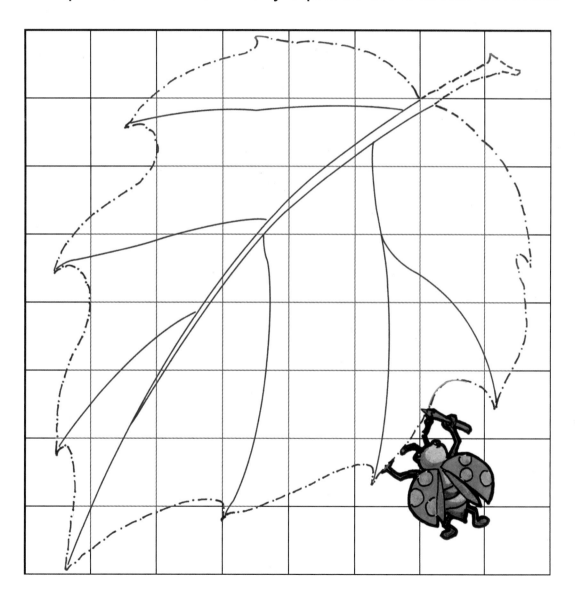

## It's time to work

1. Add up the numbers on each ball. Colour the balls according to the keys on the right.

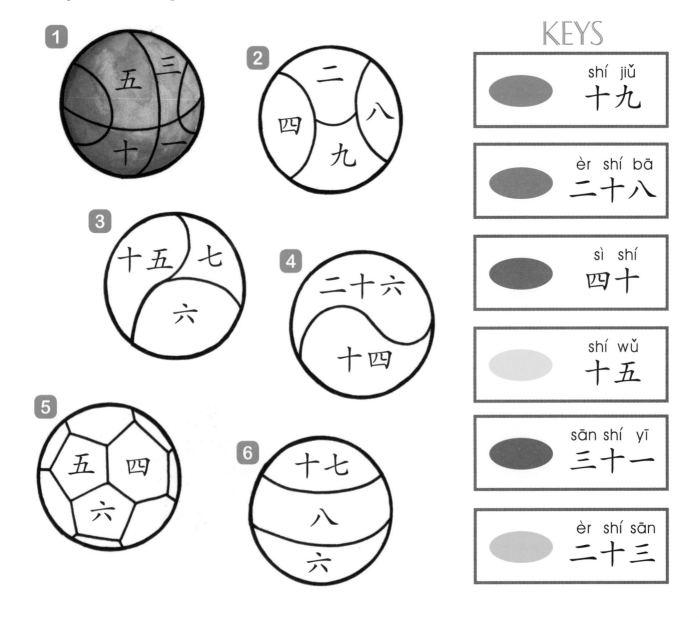

KEYS

| | |
|---|---|
| | shí jiǔ 十九 |
| | èr shí bā 二十八 |
| | sì shí 四十 |
| | shí wǔ 十五 |
| | sān shí yī 三十一 |
| | èr shí sān 二十三 |

2. Trace the lines and count up how many squares each animal has crossed to find his mother.

> **Let's learn new words**  04

① 
méi yǒu
**没有**
there isn't

② 
hé
**和**
and

③ 
yí ge
**一个**
one

④ 
liǎng ge
**两个**
two

> **Let's practise**

Say one sentence for each picture.

哥哥
我

**EXAMPLE**

wǒ yǒu yí ge gē ge
我有一个哥哥。

①

哥哥　弟弟　我

②

姐姐
妹妹
我

③

我　弟弟
弟弟

## Let's use new words

①

wǒ yǒu yí ge jiě jie hé
我有一个姐姐和

liǎng ge dì di
两个弟弟。

② 
wǒ méi yǒu jiě jie
我没有姐姐。

③

wǒ yǒu yí ge gē ge
我有一个哥哥

hé yí ge dì di
和一个弟弟。

**Let's sing** 06 他有两个弟弟

♩ = 68

我 有 一 个 姐 姐 和 一 个 妹 妹。他 有 两 个

1. 2.

弟 弟，没 有 哥 哥。 没 有 哥 哥。

## Let's say it

Say a few sentences for each picture.

**EXAMPLE**

wǒ yǒu yí ge gē ge
我有一个哥哥。

wǒ méi yǒu jiě jie
我没有姐姐。

①

②

③

Bring a photo of your brothers or sisters and introduce them to the class.

**Let's write**

1. Review the strokes.

héng zhé wān gōu

①

shù wān gōu

②

piě zhé

③

wān gōu

④

xié gōu

⑤

shù zhé zhé gōu

⑥

héng zhé gōu

⑦

2. Find the strokes and trace them with the colours given.

| jiǔ | qī | me |
|---|---|---|
| ① | ② | ③ |

| zì | wǒ | dì |
|---|---|---|
| ④ | ⑤ | ⑥ |

| liǎng | sān | shén |
|---|---|---|
| ⑦ | ⑧ | ⑨ |

| gè | bā | hé |
|---|---|---|
| ⑩ | ⑪ | ⑫ |

> **Let's play**

bà ba
爸爸

## INSTRUCTION

The children stand in a circle holding word cards. When the teacher says a word, the child with the corresponding word card should step into the centre of the circle. Any child who steps into the centre with the wrong word card will be out of the game. Continue with the activity until there is a winner.

## Some examples:

| bà ba | mā ma | dì di | mèi mei |
|-------|-------|-------|---------|
| 爸爸 | 妈妈 | 弟弟 | 妹妹 |

| gē ge | jiě jie | gǒu | māo |
|-------|---------|-----|-----|
| 哥哥 | 姐姐 | 狗 | 猫 |

| hóng sè | huáng sè |
|---------|----------|
| 红色 | 黄色 |

**Let's try it**

Match their brothers and sisters with the shadows.

①

jīng jing yǒu yí ge gē ge

京京有一个哥哥。

②

tián lì yǒu yí ge mèi mèi

田力有一个妹妹。

③

dīng yī yǒu yí ge jiě jie

丁一有一个姐姐。

④

lè le yǒu yí ge dì di

乐乐有一个弟弟。

## It's time to work

1. Match the Chinese with its meaning.

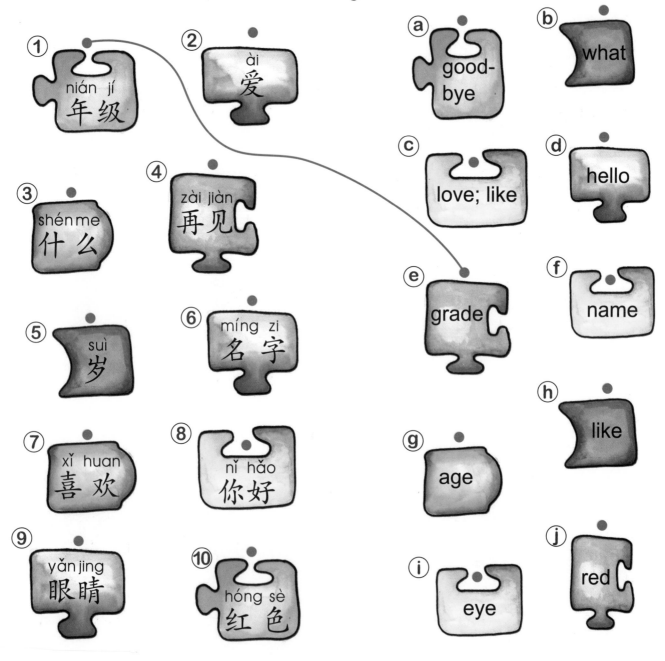

2. Match the sentences in each box with the right picture.

① wǒ yǒu yí ge gē ge
我有一个哥哥。
wǒ gē ge xǐ huan lǜ sè
我哥哥喜欢绿色。

② wǒ yǒu yí ge dì di
我有一个弟弟。
wǒ dì di ài chī pú tao
我弟弟爱吃葡萄。

③ wǒ yǒu yí ge jiě jie
我有一个姐姐。
wǒ jiě jie xǐ huan gǒu
我姐姐喜欢狗。

④ wǒ yǒu yí ge mèi mei
我有一个妹妹。
wǒ mèi mei xǐ huan chī cǎo méi
我妹妹喜欢吃草莓。

# 第三课 好朋友

**Let's learn new words** 07

①

péng you
## 朋 友
friend

②

tā
## 他
he

③

tā
## 她
she

④

shì
## 是
be

⑤

xiǎo xué shēng
## 小 学 生
primary school student

## Let's practise

Say a few sentences for each picture.

### EXAMPLE

tā yǒu yí ge péng you　　tā liù
她 有 一 个 朋 友。她 六

suì　　tā shì xiǎo xué shēng　tā
岁 。 她 是 小 学 生 。 她

shàng èr nián jí
上 二 年级。

péng you　　liù suì　　　　tā
朋 友：六岁　　　　她
xiǎo xué shēng
小 学 生
shàng èr nián jí
上 二 年级

① péng you　　qī suì　　　　tā
朋 友：七岁　　　　他
xiǎo xué shēng
小 学 生
shàng sān nián jí
上 三 年级

② péng you　　wǔ suì　　　　tā
朋 友：五岁　　　　他
xiǎo xué shēng
小 学 生
shàng yī nián jí
上 一 年级

## Let's use new words 08

田力　　　我

wǒ yǒu yí ge hǎo péng you
我 有 一 个 好 朋 友。

tā jiào tián lì　　tā shì xiǎo
他 叫 田 力。他 是 小

xué shēng
学 生。

wǒ yǒu yí ge hǎo péng you
我 有 一 个 好 朋 友。

tā jiào lè le　　tā shì xiǎo
她 叫 乐 乐。她 是 小

xué shēng
学 生。

我　　　乐乐

我有一个好朋友

我 有 一 个 好 朋 友, 好 朋 友, 他 的 名 字 叫 京 京,

叫 京 京。 京 京 是 我 的 好 朋 友, 好 朋 友。

他 是 一 个 小 学 生, 小 学 生。

## Let's say it

1. Say a few sentences about each child.

dà nián
大年

liù suì
六岁

xiǎo xué shēng
小学生

shàng èr nián jí
上 二年级

**EXAMPLE**

tā jiào dà nián     tā liù suì
他叫大年。他六岁。

tā shì xiǎo xué shēng     tā shàng
他是小学生。他 上

èr nián jí
二年级。

①

duōduo
多多

qī suì
七岁

xiǎo xué shēng
小学生

shàng sān nián jí
上 三年级

②

huān huan
欢 欢

bā suì
八岁

xiǎo xué shēng
小学生

shàng sì nián jí
上 四年级

③

lán lan
蓝蓝

bā suì
八岁

xiǎo xué shēng
小 学 生

shàng sān nián jí
上 三年级

④

xiǎo tiān
小 天

qī suì
七岁

xiǎo xué shēng
小 学 生

shàng èr nián jí
上 二年级

⑤

lì li
力力

wǔ suì
五岁

xiǎo xué shēng
小 学 生

shàng yī nián jí
上 一年级

Introduce your best friend and say a few sentences about him/ her.

## Let's write

1. Review the strokes.

piě diǎn

① 姐

héng zhé zhé piě

② 级

wò gōu

③ 您

héng piě

④ 名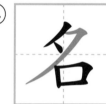

shù wān

⑤ 四

héng gōu

⑥ 你

shù tí

⑦ 眼

## 2. Find the strokes and trace them with the colours given.

| hǎo ① | fà ② | nín ③ |
| míng ④ | sì ⑤ | nǐ ⑥ |
| chī ⑦ | qī ⑧ | zì ⑨ |
| yǒu ⑩ | dì ⑪ | jiǔ ⑫ |

**Let's play**  找朋友

♩ = 67

zhǎo                                zhǎo dào
找 朋 友， 找 朋 友， 找 到 一 个  好 朋 友。
look for                            have found

你 叫 什 么 名 字? 我 叫 乐 乐, 叫 乐  乐 !

> **Let's try it**

Match the Chinese with the shadows.

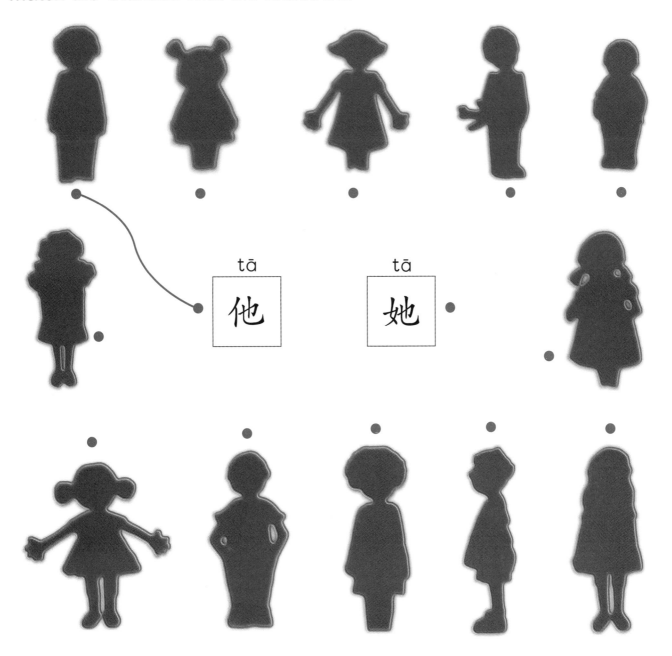

tā
他

tā
她

**It's time to work**

1. Trace all the shapes. Count up and say the number of each shape in Chinese.

十七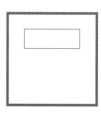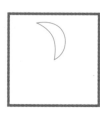

2. Trace and colour in the other half of the clown and match the Chinese with the parts of his body.

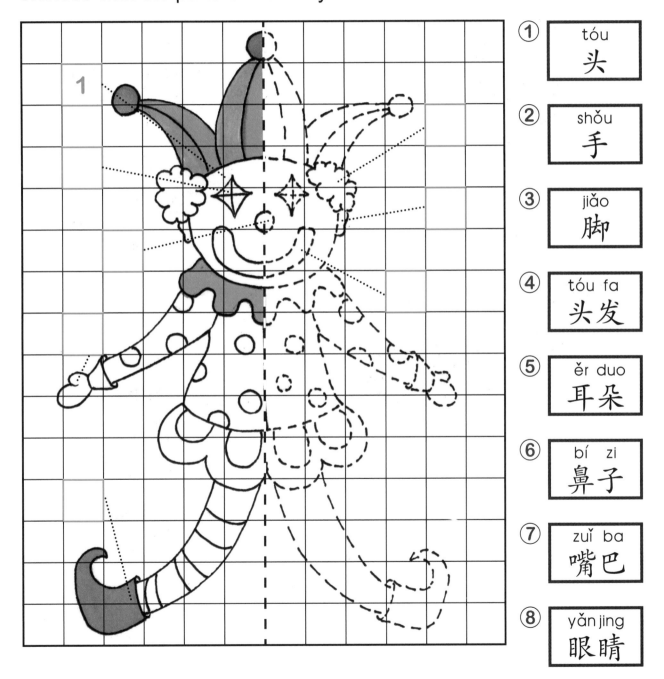

① tóu
头

② shǒu
手

③ jiǎo
脚

④ tóu fa
头发

⑤ ěr duo
耳朵

⑥ bí zi
鼻子

⑦ zuǐ ba
嘴巴

⑧ yǎn jing
眼睛

# 第四课 我的玩具

① 
wá wa
**娃娃**
doll

②
wán jù fēi jī
**玩具飞机**
toy plane

③
wán jù huǒ chē
**玩具火车**
toy train

④
wán jù xióng
**玩具熊**
teddy bear

**Let's practise**

Say one sentence for each picture.

gǒu

狗

京京

jīng jing yǒu gǒu

京京有狗。

① wán jù huǒ chē

玩具火车

田力

② wū guī

乌龟

丁一

③

wá wa

娃娃

乐乐

**Let's use new words**  12

① wǒ yǒu wá wa
我有娃娃。

丁一

② wǒ yǒu wán jù huǒ chē
我有玩具火车。

京京

③ wǒ yǒu wán jù fēi jī
我有玩具飞机。

田力

④ wǒ yǒu wán jù xióng
我有玩具熊。

乐乐

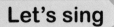   我有娃娃

我　有　娃　娃，我有玩具　熊，

我有玩具　火　车、玩具飞　机。　机。

## Let's say it

Say a few sentences for each picture.

**EXAMPLE**

<ruby>乐<rt>lè</rt></ruby> <ruby>乐<rt>le</rt></ruby> <ruby>有<rt>yǒu</rt></ruby> <ruby>爸<rt>bà</rt></ruby> <ruby>爸<rt>ba</rt></ruby>、 <ruby>妈<rt>mā</rt></ruby> <ruby>妈<rt>ma</rt></ruby>。 <ruby>她<rt>tā</rt></ruby> <ruby>有<rt>yǒu</rt></ruby> <ruby>一<rt>yí</rt></ruby> <ruby>个<rt>ge</rt></ruby> <ruby>哥<rt>gē</rt></ruby> <ruby>哥<rt>ge</rt></ruby>

<ruby>和<rt>hé</rt></ruby> <ruby>一<rt>yí</rt></ruby> <ruby>个<rt>ge</rt></ruby> <ruby>弟<rt>dì</rt></ruby> <ruby>弟<rt>di</rt></ruby>。 <ruby>乐<rt>lè</rt></ruby> <ruby>乐<rt>le</rt></ruby> <ruby>有<rt>yǒu</rt></ruby> <ruby>娃<rt>wá</rt></ruby> <ruby>娃<rt>wa</rt></ruby>。 <ruby>乐<rt>lè</rt></ruby> <ruby>乐<rt>le</rt></ruby> <ruby>的<rt>de</rt></ruby> <ruby>哥<rt>gē</rt></ruby> <ruby>哥<rt>ge</rt></ruby> <ruby>有<rt>yǒu</rt></ruby> <ruby>玩<rt>wán</rt></ruby>

<ruby>具<rt>jù</rt></ruby> <ruby>火<rt>huǒ</rt></ruby> <ruby>车<rt>chē</rt></ruby>。 <ruby>乐<rt>lè</rt></ruby> <ruby>乐<rt>le</rt></ruby> <ruby>的<rt>de</rt></ruby> <ruby>弟<rt>dì</rt></ruby> <ruby>弟<rt>di</rt></ruby> <ruby>有<rt>yǒu</rt></ruby> <ruby>玩<rt>wán</rt></ruby> <ruby>具<rt>jù</rt></ruby> <ruby>熊<rt>xióng</rt></ruby>。

爸爸 妈妈 乐乐 哥哥 弟弟

①

妹妹　田力　妈妈　爸爸　弟弟

②

爸爸　京京　妈妈　哥哥

Say a few sentences about your family.

**Let's write**

1. Learn to write Chinese characters.

> THE RULES OF WRITING CHARACTERS
> Write the strokes from top to bottom. For example, "二".

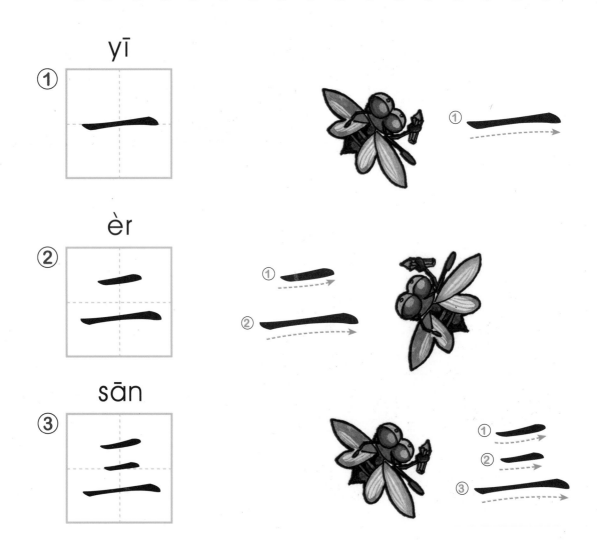

yī

èr

sān

2. Trace the *pinyin* and the characters.

| ① | | | | | |
|---|---|---|---|---|---|
| yī | yī | yī | yī | yī | yī |
| — | | | | | |

| ② | | | | | |
|---|---|---|---|---|---|
| èr | èr | èr | èr | èr | èr |
| 二 | 二 | 二 | 二 | 二 | 二 |

| ③ | | | | | |
|---|---|---|---|---|---|
| sān | sān | sān | sān | sān | sān |
| 三 | 三 | 三 | 三 | 三 | 三 |

Let's play

jiǔ
九

shí
十

二十

shí yī
十一

**INSTRUCTION**

When the teacher says a number, the children are expected to follow on. For example, when the teacher says "八", the children should say "九", "十", "十一" and so on.

Some examples:

① 八·················十六

② 二十··············三十二

③ 十四··············二十九

④ 二十八··········四十

> **Let's try it**

Count up and write down the numbers in Chinese.

①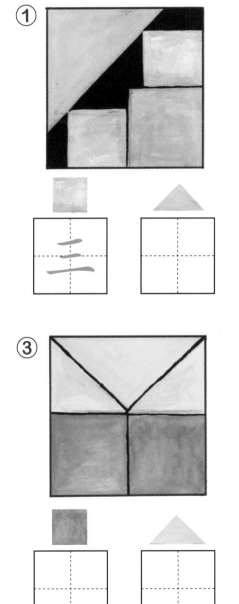

②

③ ④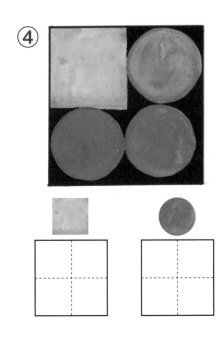

**It's time to work**

1. Fill in each space with a number according to the pattern.

## 2. Match the pictures with the Chinese and colour them in.

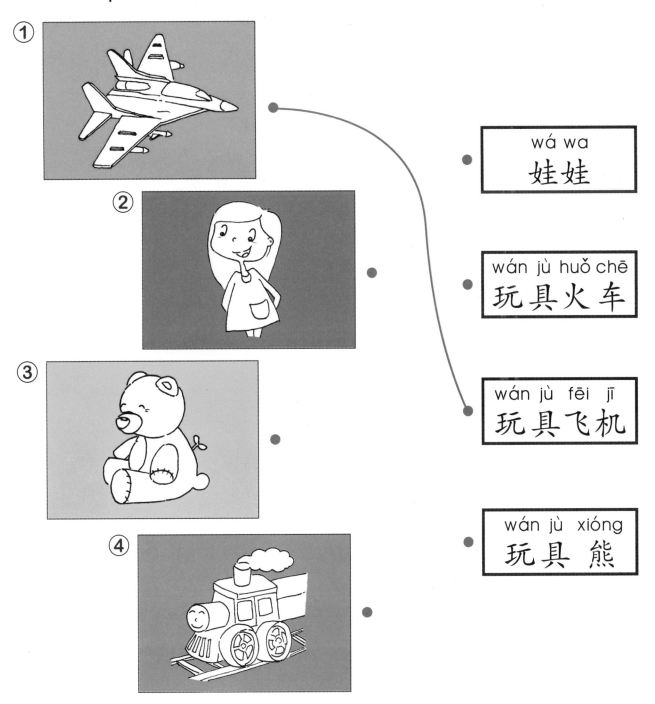

① 

② 

③ 

④ 

wá wa
娃娃

wán jù huǒ chē
玩具火车

wán jù fēi jī
玩具飞机

wán jù xióng
玩具熊

Let's learn new words

①

kàn shū
看书
read
books

②

huà huàr
画画儿
draw; paint

③

xiě zì
写字
write
characters

④

wánr yóu xì
玩儿游戏
play games

⑤

měi tiān
每天
every day

51

## Let's practise

Match the sentences with the pictures.

① tā měi tiān kàn shū
他每天看书。

② tā ài xiě zì
她爱写字。

③ tā xǐ huan huà huàr
她喜欢画画儿。

④ tā xǐ huan wánr yóu xì
他喜欢玩儿游戏。

⑤ tā xǐ huan wán jù fēi jī
他喜欢玩具飞机。

## Let's use new words 15

①

wǒ ài kàn shū

我爱看书。

②

wǒ xǐ huan huà huàr

我喜欢 画画儿。

③

wǒ xǐ huan xiě zì

我喜欢写字。

④

wǒ měi tiān wánr yóu xì

我每天玩儿游戏。

## Let's sing 🔘16 🎤 我爱看书

♩ = 68

我爱看书，　　　我爱写字，　　　我爱画画儿、

玩儿游戏。　　　　　我每天看书，每天写字，

每 天 画画儿,每 天 玩儿游 戏。

> **Let's say it**

Say one sentence about each child.

喜欢玩儿游戏

**EXAMPLE**

tián lì  xǐ huan  wánr  yóu xì
田力喜欢玩儿游戏。

田力

① 喜欢写字

丁一

② 喜欢画画儿

京京

③ 喜欢猫

乐乐

④ 喜欢狗

hóng hong
红 红

⑤ 喜欢玩具飞机

田力

⑥ 喜欢娃娃

丁一

⑦ 喜欢玩具火车

田力

⑧ 喜欢吃葡萄

péng peng
朋 朋

**Let's write**

1. Learn to write Chinese characters.

THE RULES OF WRITING CHARACTERS
Write the strokes from outside to inside before completing the character. For example, "四".

sì

① 四

wǔ

② 五

2. Trace the *pinyin* and the characters.

① 
| sì | sì | sì | sì | sì | sì |
| --- | --- | --- | --- | --- | --- |
| 四 | 四 | 四 | 四 | 四 | 四 |
| sì | sì | sì | sì | sì | sì |
| 四 | 四 | 四 | 四 | 四 | 四 |

②
| wǔ | wǔ | wǔ | wǔ | wǔ | wǔ |
| --- | --- | --- | --- | --- | --- |
| 五 | 五 | 五 | 五 | 五 | 五 |
| wǔ | wǔ | wǔ | wǔ | wǔ | wǔ |
| 五 | 五 | 五 | 五 | 五 | 五 |

Let's play

duì le
对了。
Right.

bú duì
不对。
Wrong.

shí liù jiǎn liù děng yú
十六减六等于……
minus    equal to

16 − 6 =?

十

六

**INSTRUCTION**

When the teacher says two numbers, the children are expected to find the difference and say the answer in Chinese as quickly as possible.

Some examples:

① 16 − 6 =

② 20 − 8 =

③ 30 − 5 =

④ 40 − 7 =

⑤ 20 − 15 =

⑥ 38 − 30 =

⑦ 19 − 10 =

⑧ 24 − 12 =

## Let's try it

Count up and write down the numbers in Chinese.

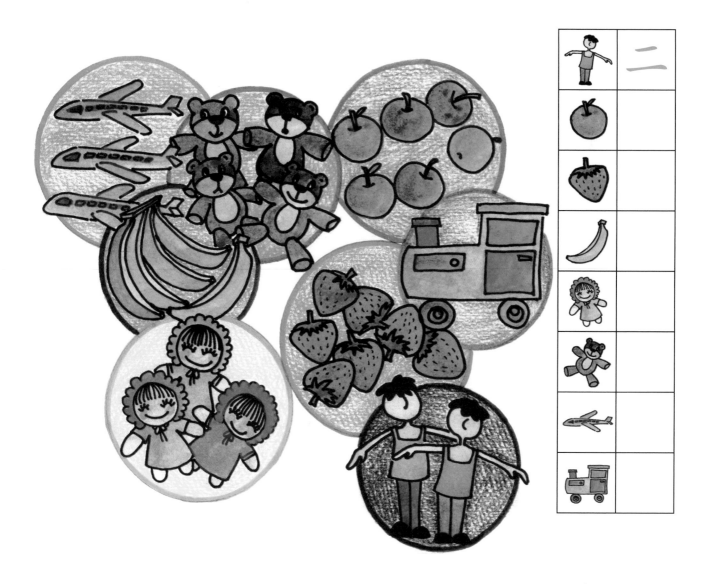

## It's time to work

1. Find five sentences following the arrows and write down their meanings.

I love reading books.

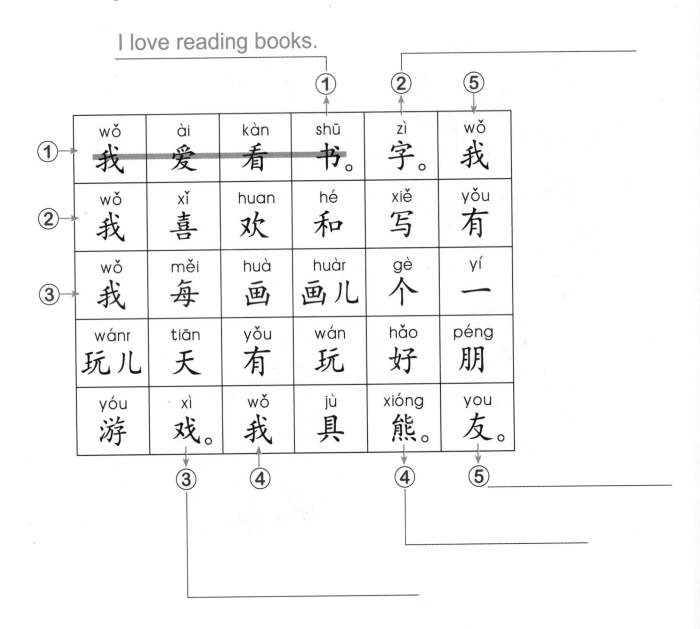

## 2. Match the pictures with the Chinese.

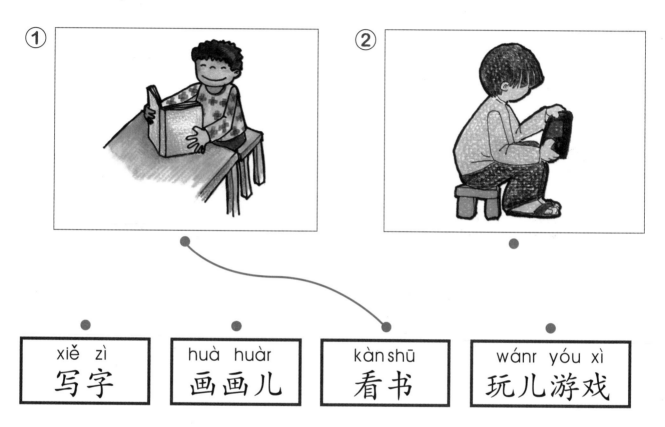

| xiě zì | huà huàr | kàn shū | wánr yóu xì |
|---|---|---|---|
| 写字 | 画画儿 | 看书 | 玩儿游戏 |

> **Let's learn new words**

① 
huì
**会**
can

② 
chuān
**穿**
put on; wear

③ 
yī fu
**衣服**
clothes

④ 
xié zi
**鞋(子)**
shoes

⑤ 
shū tóu
**梳头**
comb one's hair

⑥ 
shuā yá
**刷牙**
brush one's teeth

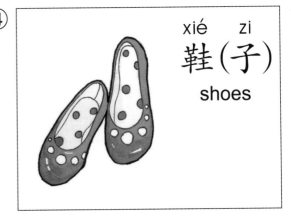

Let's practise

shuā yá
刷牙

huà huàr
画画儿

## INSTRUCTION

The class is divided into two groups. One child in each group is shown a word card by the teacher. The child is expected to act out the meaning of the word. The rest of the group are expected to say the word in Chinese. The group with more correct answers wins the game.

## Some examples:

shuā yá
刷牙

shū tóu
梳头

chuān yī fu
穿衣服

chuān xié zi
穿鞋（子）

huà huàr
画画儿

kàn shū
看书

wánr yóu xì
玩儿游戏

xiě zì
写字

> **Let's use new words**  18 ✏

①

wǒ měi tiān shuā yá
我 每 天 刷 牙。

京京

②

wǒ měi tiān shū tóu
我 每 天 梳 头。

丁一

wǒ huì chuān yī fu
我 会 穿 衣 服。

③

田力

④

wǒ huì chuān xié zi
我 会 穿 鞋(子)。

乐乐

 Let's sing 19 我每天刷牙

我每天刷牙、刷　牙。　我每天梳头、梳　头。

衣　服、衣服,我会穿。鞋子、鞋子,我会　穿。

## Let's say it

Say one sentence for each picture.

小狗

会梳头

**EXAMPLE**

xiǎo gǒu huì shū tóu
小狗会梳头。

① 丁一

喜欢写字

②

会穿衣服

小猫

③ 乌龟

会穿鞋(子)

④  喜欢玩儿游戏

田力

⑤  会刷牙

小狗

⑥ 喜欢画画儿  京京

⑦  乐乐 喜欢看书

> **Let's write**

1. Learn to write Chinese characters.

> THE RULES OF WRITING CHARACTERS
> Write the strokes from top to bottom and from left to right. For example, "六".

liù

①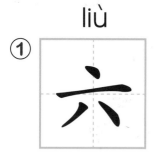

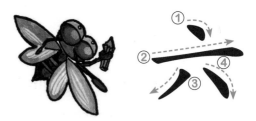

qī

②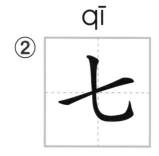

2. Trace the *pinyin* and the characters.

① 
| liù | liù | liù | liù | liù | liù |
|---|---|---|---|---|---|
| 六 | 六 | 六 | 六 | 六 | 六 |
| liù | liù | liù | liù | liù | liù |
| 六 | 六 | 六 | 六 | 六 | 六 |

② 
| qī | qī | qī | qī | qī | qī |
|---|---|---|---|---|---|
| 七 | 七 | 七 | 七 | 七 | 七 |
| qī | qī | qī | qī | qī | qī |
| 七 | 七 | 七 | 七 | 七 | 七 |

## Let's play

**INSTRUCTION**

When the teacher says a verb in Chinese, the children are expected to find a noun to match with the verb.

玩儿

yóu xì
游戏

yóu xì
游戏

zì
字

## Some examples:

| wánr yóu xì | huà huàr | kàn shū | xiě zì |
|:---:|:---:|:---:|:---:|
| 玩儿游戏 | 画画儿 | 看书 | 写字 |

| chuān xié zi | chuān yī fu | shuā yá | shū tóu |
|:---:|:---:|:---:|:---:|
| 穿鞋（子） | 穿衣服 | 刷牙 | 梳头 |

**Let's try it**

Find the route for the two related items.

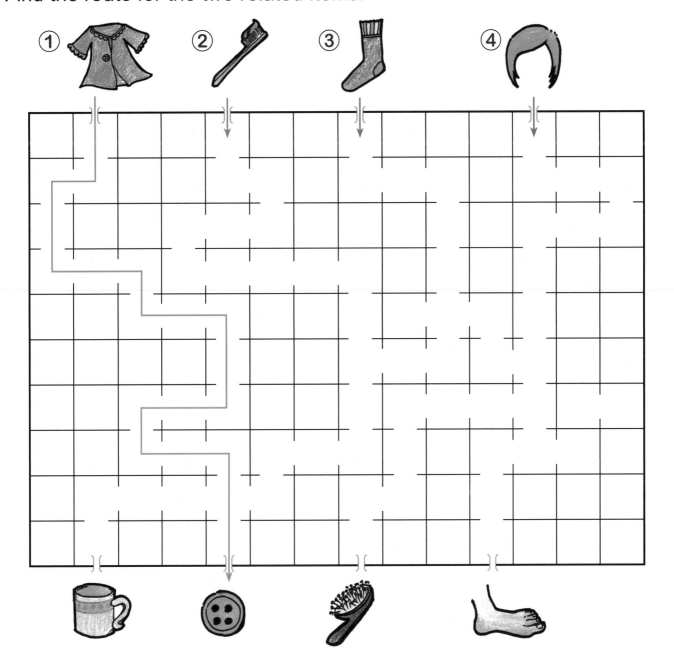

## It's time to work

1. Trace the dotted lines. Count the shapes and write down the numbers in Chinese.

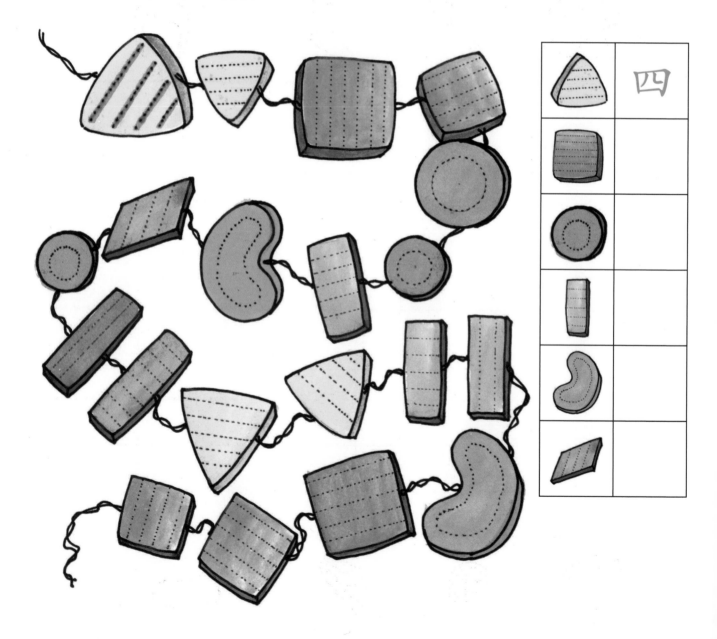

| | |
|---|---|
| shape (triangle) | 四 |
| shape (square) | |
| shape (circle) | |
| shape (rectangle) | |
| shape (bean) | |
| shape (parallelogram) | |

## 2. Match the pictures with the Chinese.

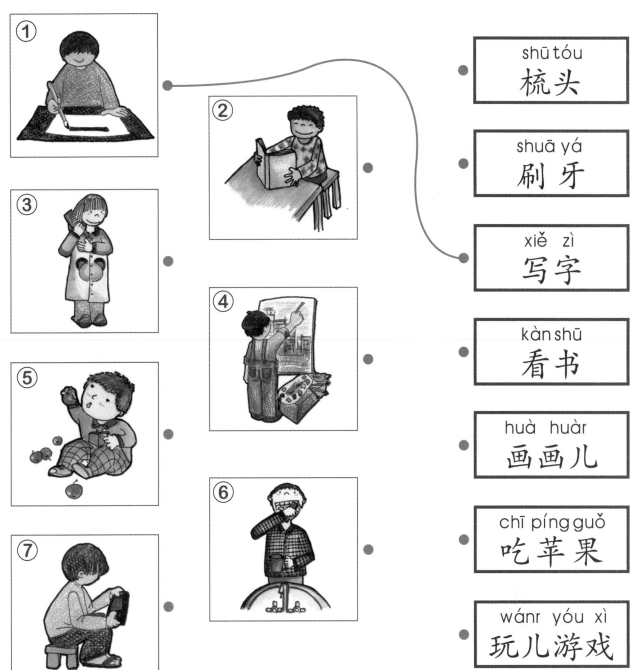

shū tóu
梳头

shuā yá
刷牙

xiě zì
写字

kàn shū
看书

huà huàr
画画儿

chī píng guǒ
吃苹果

wánr yóu xì
玩儿游戏

> **Let's learn new words**

**①**

bù
不
no

**②**

zǐ sè
紫色
purple

**③**

chéng sè
橙色
orange

**④**

fěn hóng sè
粉红色
pink

**⑤**

hēi sè
黑色
black

**⑥**

bái sè
白色
white

## Let's practise

Match the pictures with the Chinese and colour them in.

① zǐ sè de pú tao
紫色的葡萄

② huáng sè de píng guǒ
黄色的苹果

③ hēi sè de māo
黑色的猫

④ bái sè de gǒu
白色的狗

⑤ hóng sè de jīn yú
红色的金鱼

⑥ lù sè de wū guī
绿色的乌龟

⑦ chéng sè de yī fu
橙色的衣服

⑧ fěn hóng sè de xié zi
粉红色的鞋(子)

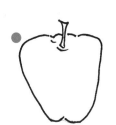

①

丁一

wǒ xǐ huan zǐ sè
我喜欢紫色。

田力

②

wǒ xǐ huan chéng sè
我喜欢 橙色。

③

wǒ xǐ huan fěn hóng sè
我喜欢粉红色。

乐乐

④ 京京

wǒ bù xǐ huan hēi sè hé bái sè
我不喜欢黑色和白色。

   我喜欢紫色

♩= 66

紫 色、紫 色，我 喜 欢。橙 色、橙 色，我 喜 欢。

粉红色、粉红色，我喜欢。黑色、白色，我 不喜欢。

**Let's say it**

Colour in the clown according to the information below. Describe the clown in Chinese.

tā yǒu
他有：

chéng sè de tóu fa
橙色的头发、

lán sè de yǎn jing
蓝色的眼睛、

hóng sè de bí zi
红色的鼻子、

fěn hóng sè de zuǐ ba
粉红色的嘴巴、

lǜ sè de shǒu
绿色的手。

tā chuān
他穿：

zǐ sè de yī fu
紫色的衣服、

hēi sè de xié zi
黑色的鞋(子)。

tā chuān zǐ sè de yī fu
他穿 紫色的衣服。

tā yǒu chéng sè de tóu fa
他有 橙色的头发。

## Let's write

1. Learn to write Chinese characters.

> **THE RULES OF WRITING CHARACTERS**
> First write the horizontal stroke and then the vertical one. For example, "十".

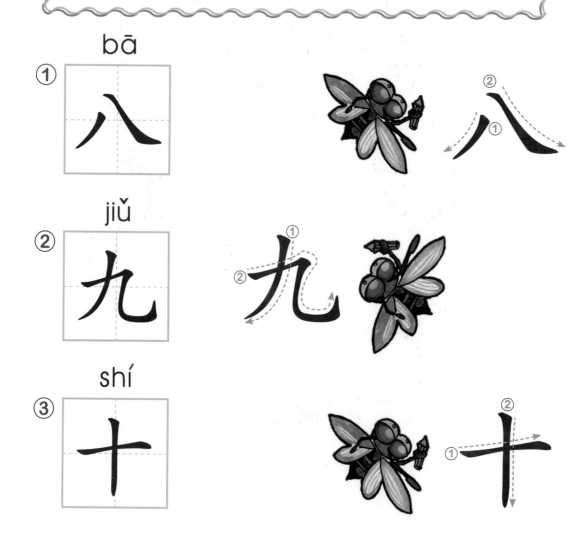

bā
① 八

jiǔ
② 九

shí
③ 十

2. Trace the *pinyin* and the characters.

① | bā | bā | bā | bā | bā | bā |
| 八 | 八 | 八 | 八 | 八 | 八 |

② | jiǔ | jiǔ | jiǔ | jiǔ | jiǔ | jiǔ |
| 九 | 九 | 九 | 九 | 九 | 九 |
| jiǔ | jiǔ | jiǔ | jiǔ | jiǔ | jiǔ |
| 九 | 九 | 九 | 九 | 九 | 九 |

③ | shí | shí | shí | shí | shí | shí |
| 十 | 十 | 十 | 十 | 十 | 十 |

**Let's play**

hóng sè de píng guǒ
红色的苹果

hóng sè
红色

píngguǒ
苹果

## Some examples:

| hóng sè | lán sè | lǜ sè | huáng sè | hēi sè | chéng sè |
|---|---|---|---|---|---|
| 红色 | 蓝色 | 绿色 | 黄色 | 黑色 | 橙色 |

| fěn hóng sè | zǐ sè | pú tao | yī fu | xié zi | yǎn jing |
|---|---|---|---|---|---|
| 粉红色 | 紫色 | 葡萄 | 衣服 | 鞋(子) | 眼睛 |

| tóu fa | píng guǒ | wū guī | xiāng jiāo |
|---|---|---|---|
| 头发 | 苹果 | 乌龟 | 香蕉 |

## Let's try it

Add up and write down the sums in Chinese. Colour in the sections according to the keys on the right.

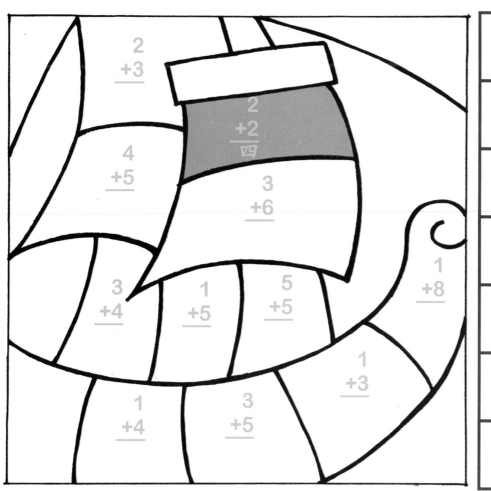

KEYS

| | |
|---|---|
| sì | hóng sè |
| 四: | 红色 |
| wǔ | lán sè |
| 五: | 蓝色 |
| liù | lù sè |
| 六: | 绿色 |
| qī | huáng sè |
| 七: | 黄色 |
| bā | chéng sè |
| 八: | 橙色 |
| jiǔ | zǐ sè |
| 九: | 紫色 |
| shí | hēi sè |
| 十: | 黑色 |

> **It's time to work**

1. Count up and write down the numbers in Chinese.

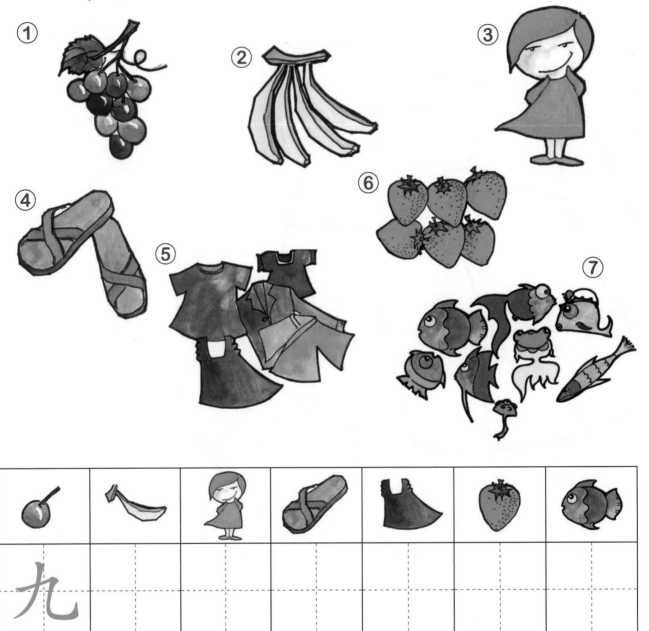

2. Colour in the pictures according to the keys on the right.

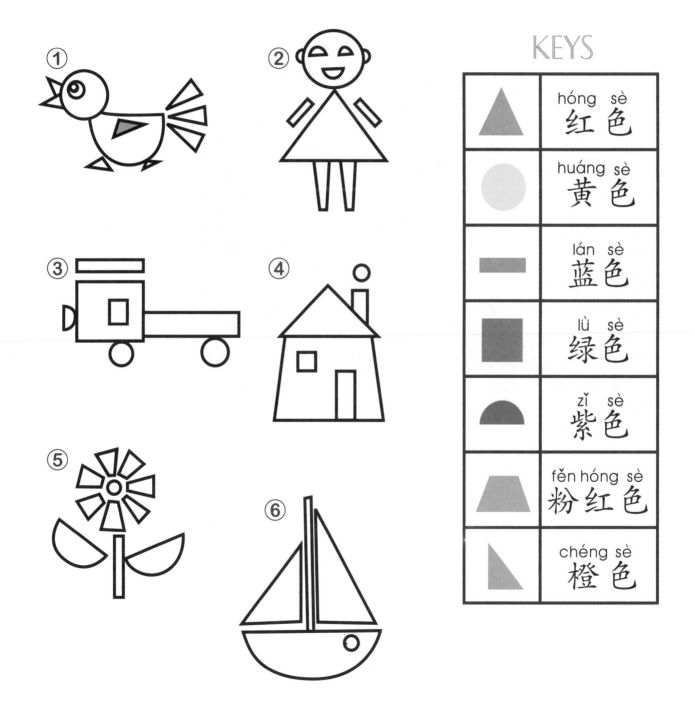

## 年的故事 The story of *Nian*

In ancient times, there was a monster called *Nian* who lived in the mountains. Towards the end of winter when there was nothing to eat, it would visit the villages and attack and eat whatever it could. The villagers would live in terror over the winter. Over time, the villagers realized that *Nian* was afraid of 3 things: the colour red, fire and noise. The villagers agreed that when *Nian* came again, they would start a fire in front of every gate, hang up red-coloured couplets on every gate, and make loud noises. One night when *Nian* came down, saw the fire and heard the noise, it freaked out and ran into the mountains and never returned. The next morning, people got up, congratulated each other and had a big celebration. Thus the custom of *"guonian"* (celebrating the New Year) was established.

Colour in the picture.

B

Find the stickers on Page D and put them at the right places.

nián de gù shi
年的故事 The story of *Nian*

C

You will be awarded with a sticker when a piece of good work is completed.

Put the stickers below at the right places on page C.

# 词汇表 VOCABULARY

## Lesson 1

| 二十六 | èrshíliù | twenty-six |
| 三十八 | sānshíbā | thirty-eight |
| 四十 | sìshí | forty |
| 加 | jiā | plus |
| 等于 | děngyú | equal to |

## Lesson 2

| 没有 | méiyǒu | there isn't |
| 和 | hé | and |
| 一个 | yí ge | one |
| 两个 | liǎng ge | two |

## Lesson 3

| 朋友 | péngyou | friend |
| 他 | tā | he |
| 她 | tā | she |
| 是 | shì | be |
| 小学生 | xiǎoxuéshēng | primary school student |

| 找 | zhǎo | look for |
| 找到 | zhǎodào | have found |

## Lesson 4

| 娃娃 | wáwa | doll |
| 玩具飞机 | wánjù fēijī | toy plane |
| 玩具火车 | wánjù huǒchē | toy train |
| 玩具熊 | wánjù xióng | teddy bear |

## Lesson 5

| 看书 | kàn shū | read books |
| 画画儿 | huà huàr | draw; paint |
| 写字 | xiě zì | write characters |
| 玩儿游戏 | wánr yóuxì | play games |
| 每天 | měitiān | every day |
| 减 | jiǎn | minus |
| 对了 | duì le | right |
| 不对 | bú duì | wrong |

## Lesson 6

| | | |
|---|---|---|
| 会 | huì | can |
| 穿 | chuān | put on; wear |
| 衣服 | yīfu | clothes |
| 鞋(子) | xié (zi) | shoes |
| 梳头 | shū tóu | comb one's hair |
| 刷牙 | shuā yá | brush one's teeth |

## Lesson 7

| | | |
|---|---|---|
| 不 | bù | no |
| 紫色 | zǐsè | purple |
| 橙色 | chéngsè | orange |
| 粉红色 | fěnhóngsè | pink |
| 黑色 | hēisè | black |
| 白色 | báisè | white |